ANCHOR BOOKS

Weeny Wonders
Edited by Neil Day

First published in Great Britain in 2000 by
ANCHOR BOOKS
Remus House,
Coltsfoot Drive,
Peterborough, PE2 9JX
Telephone (01733) 898102

All Rights Reserved

Copyright Contributors 2000

HB ISBN 1 85930 861 9
SB ISBN 1 85930 866 X

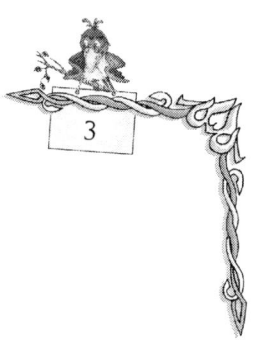

Foreword

The challenge was set within these pages - to write a story with a beginning, a middle and an end in only fifty words. And so the Mini-Saga was born. Lots are said in a few words enabling a brief exchange between both reader and writer, yet ultimately creating a stronger bond as characters and stories unfold between the lines. Read on to enjoy the very best in a huge variety of stories, tales, sagas and fables, sure to demand and delight all who read within.

Neil Day, Editor

Contents

Baby's First Outing	Lesley Edwards	10
The Way She Went	Heather Millichap	11
And The Can Of Worms Was Opened And...	Wendy Jackson	12
Greek Mythology - Persephone And...	Laura Harris	13
Set Me Free	Vanessa Hearnden	14
Fatal Pursuit	Kaylie Reakes	15
Evil Creatures	Annabel Reynolds	16
Jason And The Golden Fleece - The...	Jennifer Webb	17
In The Beginning Or How One Wrong Answer...	Anne Chamberlin	18
Haunted By Shadows From An Empty House...	Audrey Allen	19
An Affair Of The Heart	Pam Redmond	20
Overboard	Kate McDonnell	21
Circus	Emily Sayers	22
Reign Of Brutality	Angus Alexander Brown	23
Searching For The Lamp	Victoria Hemmings	24
The Mystical Piper	James Parkinson	25
Prometheus And The Little People	Chris Williams	26
The Seeds That Changed My Life	Catherine Drew	27
Trojan	Adam Jones	28
Their Time	Jack Adams	29
The Gift	Thomas Bristow	30
Baa Baa Black Sheep - What They Don't...	Claire Thurlow	31
Atlanta's Race	Michael Warner	32
Atlanta's Race	Harriet Moore	33
Rumpelstiltskin	Nicola Warren	34
A Different Kind Of Weaver	Katie Brown	35
The Web-Spinning Weaver	Katy Denton	36
A Date With Vertebrate?	John Evans	37
Trials Of The Dawn	Marylène Walker	38
Love	Danielle Gallagher	39
Black Or Blue	Roger Foster	40
Always Let Your Conscience Be Your Guide!	Margaret Franklin	41
War Wounds	Anne Smithers	42
Twilight Mystery	Angus Alexander Brown	43

The Maize And The Minotaur	Joanna Sinclair	44
Mini-Saga	Emma Chandley	45
Under New Management	Lesley Grewer	46
A Day To Celebrate	Elizabeth Myra Crellin	47
Saved	Marian Hunt	48
I'm A Doll	Mary Duffy	49
Heartbeats Race My Footsteps	John L Wright	50
Man Of Vision	Ron Beaton	51
The Warrior King	David Rosser	52
The Old Tweed Jacket	Cyril Mountjoy	53
The Year 2050	Ann Hathaway	54
The Saga Of The Flight Of The Eagle	Bill Hayles	55
Robin Hood And The King	Keith Powell	56
Time Warp	Jean Paisley	57
A Reflection No More	Helen Jones	58
The Wicker Chair	G Wright	59
The Next Step	Perry McDaid	60
Hotel Room	Andrew Detheridge	61
Princess Diana	Laura Beckett	62
The Concert	Kirsten Shea	63
The Robot	Natalie Mair	64
The Haunted Mansion	R Fenech	65
Who Would Win?	Adam Mullins	66
Destiny	Tony Coyle	67
Distant Dreams Or Memories? I Will Never Know!	Frank E Trickett	68
Atlantis Boy	Clive MacDonald	69
Big Adventure 2000	Chris Payne	70
The Car	Philip Hawkins	71
Soccer Legend	Aden Philpott	72
Heading For The Line	Luke Avron-Cotton	73
The Lake	Richard Barling	74
From Riches To Rags	Darren Armstrong	75
Champion	Paul Gregory	76
It's A Knockout	Michael Godden	77
The Submarine	Daniel Howard	78
The Race	Jacob Brown	79

The Gunman	Gary Sandy	80
Flying Needle	Jane Noble	81
The Jump	Carl O'Neill	82
The Winner And The Loser	Willlam Lay	83
Blade And Blood	Andrew Dickson	84
Is He The One?	Andrew Dickson	85
Untitled	Alison McKibben	86
The Great Battle	Karen McKee	87
Untitled	Sarah McVeigh	88
Fire	Elilzabeth Patterson	89
Short Story	Gemma Mornin	90
The Race	Anne-Marie Pier	91
The Test	Holly Neilson	92
I Wonder	Lucy Vanes	93
No More	April Rose	94
Mini-Saga	Emma Boyce	95
Lost And Found	Joanna Moore	96
Mini-Saga	Haylety Mackin	97
Love Never Dies	Dawn Snelling	98
One-Eyed Sally	Laura Brown	99
Mini-Saga	Elisa Battista	100
The Storm	Gemma White	101
The Race	Jesse Ryan	102
The Ghost Story With Another Sense of . . .	Stephanie Calvely	103
The Lonely Boy	Rachel McKnight	104
The Boy Who Fell From The Sky And Landed . . .	Clare Forehead	105
Living In America	Paul Gault	106
My Tenth Birthday	Nicola Gibb	107
Keeping My Cool	Jessica Campbell	108
The Stealing Orphan	Manbir Singh	109
101 Dalmations	Louise Edwards	110
Tornado	David Breakell	111
We Can Live Twenty-One Days Without Food . . .	Glen Thomas	112
Hostage	Tom Ralph	113

The Mini-Sagas

Baby's First Outing

Settling little Molly into her pram had been easy, dappled sun shone through leaves onto tiny hands as the new wheels bumped along the canal path.

Karen heard footsteps hurrying behind,
then the social worker's words,
'She's not your baby!'

Karen smiled and a siren wailed as the pram sank.

Lesley Edwards

The Way She Went

Every night, a sea of golden threads surrounded her angelic face. However, this night, her head had been engulfed by a swamp of red juice.

Her features were blurred and her delicate soul destroyed.

Her cold body lay still and her spirit flew up to the golden gates of Heaven.

Heather Millichap

And The Can Of Worms Was Opened And The Green Liquid Poured Out

I had a clear picture of an old shaped bottle of emerald green liquid.
Stopped with a brownish cork.

Against it stood a dirty old baked-bean tin without the lid.
The worms had already started to come out.

The contents in the green liquid bottle was called *Hurt*.

Wendy Jackson

Greek Mythology - Persephone And The Pomegranate Seeds

Hunger is a dangerous thing: In this case it led to everlasting misery. Six insignificant pomegranate seeds that locked her destiny in place and forced her to live in the barren underworld. Kidnapped by Pluto, hunger overcame her defiance. Persephones last hope was Zeus, God above all Gods.

Laura Harris

Set Me Free

Day after day I was incarcerated.
No way out,
No light!
As the key turned in the lock . . .
Out leapt pain, cruelty and death.

All happiness was over
The lid's closing in
No!
I must get out, I am hope!
Pandora couldn't resist temptation.
Now darkness is upon us . . .

Vanessa Hearnden (14)

An Anchor Books Anthology

Fatal Pursuit

They were gaining ground, but running faster just cramped my legs. I felt the sweat trickling down my face as I turned a sharp corner off the long twisting alley. They carried on without noticing me. My hand felt strange, I lifted it. I had it, I had the disease!

Kaylie Reakes (14)

Evil Creatures

There it is. The box. I want to open it, but I mustn't.

I want to. There can't be any harm in taking a peek, can there?

'Let us out' ask the voices again. My hand stretches towards the box. Shaking fingers close on it. I open . . .

Uh oh!

Annabel Reynolds

17

Jason And The Golden Fleece - The Clashing Cliffs' Challenge

I saw the cliffs approach our ship, clashing together, the valley echoed a deafening roar as the fire and sparks flew up. But it was Jason's destiny to reach the golden fleece. He took a deep breath and disappeared under the churning sea leaving only dust and smoke behind him.

Jennifer Webb

In The Beginning Or How One Wrong Answer Changed The Course Of History

The journey was long and hard. On the donkey's back the woman felt the child clamour within her. Lantern lights showed the inn ahead.

'Is there any room'?

'Yes.'

A star led kings to an empty stable. Shepherds found no one to worship. There was no Light of the World.

Anne Chamberlin

An Anchor Books Anthology

Haunted By Shadows From An Empty House - Why Do They Haunt Me?

The house is empty now, yet late at night, I see the lights. Their shadows, dancing to the music they all loved, before that fatal night. When two cars met in a terrible crash, that took their music away. Why did I wish so hard, for the music to stop?

Audrey Allen

An Affair Of The Heart

She looked down at the coffin.
Unexpected, her husband's death.
A quiet man, though once garrulous she remembered,
full of silly ideas, like working abroad.
Who wants to leave England?

Strange how their son had gone to Australia.

She read the death certificate again:
'Cause of death - a broken heart'.

Pam Redmond

Overboard

The breeze was refreshing as they steamed through the night. There were many noises - engines, generators, fans. He leaned on the rail savouring his cigar.

The rail gave. He was overboard. Surfacing he saw the ship disappearing. He knew he would die. He was right. The sharks converged upon him.

Kate McDonnell

Circus

The dog stepped up to jump through the ring of fire. He saw flames leaping in front of him. He built up all his strength and ran forward, then he jumped, through the flames and out on the other side. He had done it for the first time ever.

Emily Sayers

Reign Of Brutality

The Warden's door slammed shut. Transfer denied again . . . but why?

All week I paced my cell, racking my brain. But no answers. Solitary confinement followed - so did the beatings!

Months later, recovering in Intensive Care, I was approached by the Warden. Looking down at me, he sneered: 'Comply or die.'

Angus Alexander Brown

Searching For The Lamp

I stopped dead in my tracks. 'What the hell was that?' I muttered fearfully under my breath. I heard a loud thunderous rumble, the cave was collapsing around me. My hands fumbled around in the darkness. Trembling from head to foot, I searched for the lamp.

Victoria Hemmings

The Mystical Piper

The Major should have listened, he should have paid up but it was too late. He had driven him too far. Off went the mystical flute player playing a magical tune. If only the Major had known. It was all his fault, the children were never to be seen again.

James Parkinson

Prometheus And The Little People

Chained to the rock, damned to torture by the callous eagles.
Zeus felt sorry for him. He was tormenting the feeble. With one
great strike of his pliers of lightning, he set Prometheus free and
put him back to concentrate on the little people.

Chris Williams

The Seeds That Changed My Life

He snatched my waist, I couldn't breathe. The Chariot raced off once again. I desired to go home.
'But we shall be so happy together . . . now eat something,' he said, discarding twelve seeds into my hands.

I devoured six seeds, but little did I know,
I had become his prisoner!

Catherine Drew

Trojan

'It's a tribute to Troy!' they shouted,
'We've won!' they cheered.
'The fools, they've fallen for it, I can't believe they could be so naive!' whispered Odysseus, excitement in his tone.

Night fell, the time had arrived. 'Open it on my command!' They unbolted the hidden door and leapt out.

Adam Jones (13)

Their Time

It was noisy outside. The men were still crouched down, scared into a deadly silence, for if they made a sound, the men would be no more.

It was quiet now, the partying had stopped. They prepared themselves, for now they would settle their fates, once and for all.

Jack Adams (13)

The Gift

They could hear the voices of the Trojans outside, some said, 'It's a tribute to Troy!' Others believed that it was a trick. Even so, the people of Troy didn't listen. Instead they celebrated, when the last person had fallen asleep, a door opened in the stomach of the horse.

Thomas Bristow (14)

Baa Baa Black Sheep - What They Don't Tell You At Nursery School!

The search for the wool had turned from a mundane occupation to a compulsive obsession. The farmer needed wool. He knew the little boy who lived down the lane was not a patient child. He neared the horrified sheep who was hatching an escape route, there was no way out!

Claire Thurlow

Atlanta's Race

His lungs were on fire, every step he took, she took two and she was soon streaking ahead again, the crowd shouted willing him to win, as he was too young to die. He threw the last golden apple. She glanced at the two in her hands and smiled.

Michael Warner

Atlanta's Race

The race against her,
Would leave any man out of breath,
But when they lose,
Are greeted by death.
Hipponenes wanted Atlanta
And cried to Venus,
'Oh how I love her!'
Venus gave Hipponenes apples of gold
And Atlanta ate,
Hipponenes won the race
And they married with haste.

Harriet Moore (14)

Rumpelstiltskin

A miller, whose daughter was beautiful had lied about her and the king heard she could turn straw into gold. The king locked her away with some straw. She was very upset, he said he would kill her. Suddenly there was tapping, and a little man came through the keyhole.

Nicola Warren (14)

A Different Kind Of Weaver

Even before I started, I knew I had won the competition. Athene was nowhere near as good as I was. When I won, Athene agreed that I was best, but I was too arrogant.

Now, I still weave but my work is unappreciated as I am a spider.

Katie Brown

The Web-Spinning Weaver

Arachne took in all the compliments, she was outstanding and she knew it, she even said she could conquer the Goddess Athene. Athene agreed she was the greatest needlewoman, but being too conceited was her downfall so she turned her into the best web-spinning woman around. Yes a spider!

Katy Denton

A Date With Vertebrate?

I cast a line deep beneath the surge,
with a baited hook on the bottom, for it's the seabed I purge.
Before I fish the sea, for bait I often dig,
and as for the one that got away, to the wife I say 'It was this big.'

John Evans

Trials Of The Dawn

Patiently, the darkness says goodbye with the shyness of a caterpillar afraid to fly. But the sun tears the journey of the stars. First class moon, the daylight robs her of the cigars she keeps unlit to plead her case. Who can prove the good intentions of my dreams?

Marylène Walker

Love

Love is a smile, a tear, a touch,
love says so little but means so much.
Love is forever and I give it to you,
From the one who thinks the world of you.

Danielle Gallagher

Black Or Blue

The pirate ship lays off shore, plundering lags row away from the remote island's sandy beach. Their booty seemingly secured. The heavy drinking and laughing turned to terror as their ship exploded into raging flames, a thousands miles from civilisation, a thousand yards from chanting spear-waving savages on shore.

Roger Foster

Always Let Your Conscience Be Your Guide!

Three lads went tomato-picking but the crop failed. Penniless they were shipped home.

'Next visit you must repay the fare,' intoned the Jersey policeman. Forty-seven years later, on a day trip, Peter dutifully offered money in St Helier's police station.
'The obligation was waived after three years,' grinned the bemused officer.

Margaret Franklin

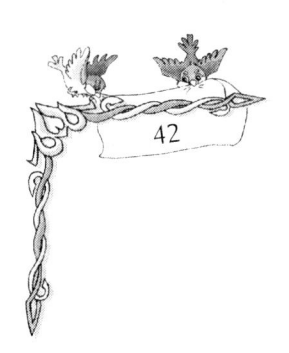

War Wounds

The eleventh hour, eleventh day, peace at last and my Jack killed the day afterwards.
News of peace hadn't reached the front lines and I'm left with gallantry medals and a wedding dress that has languished in tissue for four lonely years.
I'm bitterly angry at Fate's Eleventh hour cheating victory.

Anne Smithers

Twilight Mystery

Sitting peacefully on my veranda at sunset, I suddenly spy movement at the woodland's edge. Venturing forth, I gently pad across lawn, then wildflower meadow.

I come to a halt, staring into shadow - then gasp, when out of the twilight wood steps a beautiful maiden with rainbows in her eyes.

Angus Alexander Brown

The Maze And The Minotaur

I paused,
All I could hear was the *thumping* irregular
beat of my heart,
I carried on,
Surrounded by a cloak of darkness
My only accompaniment,
My ragged breathing and the
eerie hum of silence.
Something rough brushed past my fingers,
I dropped the twine.
My mind went *blank*.

Joanna Sinclair

Mini-Saga

She receives the ball from the halfway mark, dribbles it past the dog invading the pitch. A beautiful turn there, she stops at nothing, she takes on the keeper, she shoots, she scores! The ball hits the front of the shed. The garden goes wild, Michael Owen eat your heart out!

Emma Chandley

Under New Management

They came.
A first viewing showed it had potential, but needed a lot of building work doing, not to mention the plumbing. There were some administrative problems to sort out and the locals were not happy, but these were conquered.

In due course the Romans left Britain.

Lesley Grewer

A Day To Celebrate

Excitement compelled us to leave home earlier than necessary.
It was our filly's first appearance on the racecourse.
We had high hopes she would be first past the post.
She paraded round the paddock on her toes.
And went on to win a cracking race.

Congratulations rang out.
Cheers.

Elizabeth Myra Crellin

Saved

*(A weekend away looked like fun.
Little did they know what lay ahead . . .!)*

A group of young Christians were attending a conference.

Excitingly looking forward to meeting friends tomorrow, they tumbled into bed.

New day dawned, and after breakfast, the minister received an alarming message . . . Jean had lost her soul!

However, the milkman saved the day by repairing the *sole* of her shoes.

Marian Hunt

I'm A Doll

I'm sad, sad, I say is there anyone listening? I can't see straight. No one loves me - no one cares. I'm all confused. What's happening? I can't even think, as someone lifts me up and calls me a doll.
I realise that she's right.

Mary Duffy

Heartbeats Race My Footsteps

I hate my situation, this room is bare and cold. I am alone and
afraid. Another awaits with a more comfortable chair. No rent to
pay - but I must. It is time. I walk the few paces, I sit securely.
Others peer.
A switch is thrown. I am at peace!

John L Wright

Man Of Vision

'Of all the hair-brained ideas you have produced to date, this one excels them all' said his friends.

'A flying machine that can move vertically and horizontally under its own power!'

Undeterred, Leonardo de Vinci rolled up his design and slipped it back in its drawer.

Ron Beaton

The Warrior King

The warrior ran a million miles
And then came the sunrise
The castle was standing big and strong
And then with a sound of a *gong* it was gone!

He rested with his shield and his spear
And whispered to the crowd that was near
Ho'dear, King Lear!

David Rosser

The Old Tweed Jacket

Grandad's Harris tweed jacket hung in the hall, his pride and joy for a few years. Worn and frayed a comfort for outside chores for much longer. Mum sent it to the jumble sale. He bought it back. He's been gone two years. His jacket still hangs in the hall.

Cyril Mountjoy

The Year 2050

Huddled in a cave, by firelight, Annabella, a deaf mute, watched her father draw pictures with his hands, trying to explain why they were the only people left on earth.

Birds flew high in heaven dropping massive eggs that exploded destroying everything on earth.
Only they survived.

Ann Hathaway

The Saga Of The Flight Of The Eagle

The mighty Titan Apollo rose into the heavens, bearing the three brave explorers, their destination . . . Moon.
With the power of a million horses the Luna Chariot was propelled, for three days they traversed the blackness of space and conquering that lifeless ord in the name of Humanity, returned triumphantly Home.

Bill Hayles

Robin Hood And The King

Robin Hood and all his merry men were sat around the camp fire, having a good chat about the king, was he back in England after all? There had been reports of him being seen around the Derby area but nobody was quite sure about the facts, it was a very late night.

Keith Powell

Time Warp

The children clapped, a clown tumbled about and made them laugh.

Sadie ran up ramps right to the roof to slide all the way down.

She slipped inside the giant plastic tube but, when she came back out it was all grey. The air was smoky, time had gone away.

Jean Paisley

A Reflection No More

He stood there lapping the velvet water, a reflection of black and orange entwined stared back, golden amber eyes penetrated hard, creamy white surrounding his face. Ears alert, but not enough.

The hunter steps in, pupils dilated of the prey.

Bang!

The reflection of the tiger no longer remains.

Helen Jones (14)

The Wicker Chair

A long month for the young pilot, August 1940. Awake each
dawn, yet tired still, he sat in his wicker chair at the field.
Scramble bell ringing his call to arms.
Spitfire now climbing into the sun, will his battle ever be done?
Next day the wicker chair remained empty.

G Wright

The Next Step

He awoke, senses alive to each wonder this new existence presented - effortlessly speeding through the air, skimming deliciously cool invigorating waters - flitting about, frenziedly ingesting each new beauty. Life had been tedium, heaven was astounding. The mayfly embraced approaching darkness as another joy, yet puzzled over the terrible weakness.

Perry McDaid

Hotel Room

In room twenty-one, she sat alone in the only chair, thinking nothing as the last minutes of her life slipped away. She had wanted for nothing: beautiful house, husband, three children, holidays abroad. But, what had she achieved herself? Nothing, she concluded, as the pills scattered on the floor.

Andrew Detheridge

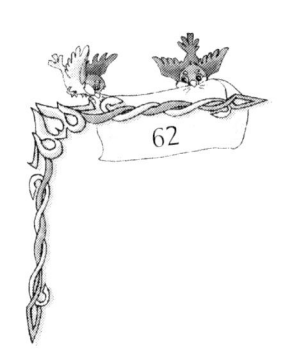

Princess Diana

A silence spread among her people.
Tears fell as they whispered their goodbyes.
They promised themselves that she would never be forgotten.
She wasn't.
The spirit of Princess Diana lives on.

Laura Beckett (13)

The Concert

With pounding heart she acknowledged the instant and rapturous applause, as the sounds of her flute faded. And as the clapping grew to a crescendo, it sounded like music to her ears. This was her first experience as a soloist, and with exhilaration, she realised, it wouldn't be her last.

Kirsten Shea

The Robot

I pressed the *start* button, and my new invention sprang to life. *Hisssss!* With a cloud of smoke and a bang of light, my creation fell to the ground in a heap. I had failed. My metal friend had gone, disappeared, vanished, died. There he lay, still, lifeless. Oh dear!

Natalie Mair (9)

The Haunted Mansion

I climbed the stairs of the haunted mansion, followed by the parish priest. Suddenly, drawers from a wardrobe started flying in our direction. The place was empty. There was only the sound of thunder in the distance. What was I supposed to say in my article - that ghosts don't exist?

R Fenech

Who Would Win?

It was the biggest race of the year. Everyone on edge. Most thought they would know who would win, but the excitement was the key. The race was going to be long and hard, the racers were confident. One racer thought he was too good but the turtle beat the hare.

Adam Mullins (13)

Destiny

He was going to die;
Lusted for it.
The atmosphere was intense.
He rose,
The crowd went wild.
Cheering, applauding, stamping;
Afraid.
He was arrogant, imperious:
He draped the purple robe
Across his shoulders.
Gods trembled!
He shouted,
Octavian is dead!
Augustus is born!
The crowd screamed
'Hail Caesar!'

Tony Coyle

Distant Dreams Or Memories? I Will Never Know!

I had lain in hospital a long time, with many visitors. At last I was going home. Going through all the motions of movements, was I dreaming? Passing by many smiling faces in lights and darkness. Then one shining light and I was no more.
My end I think!

Frank E Trickett

Atlantis Boy

The near-naked youth perched upon the rock. He watched as overalled men raked foam scoured into the black shoreline. People such as these, pillaged every ocean searching out his watery world. Fearing capture, he scuttled into the odourless sea, outward and down to dancing bladderwrack and a thousand myths.

Clive MacDonald

Big Adventure 2000

I was running through haunted mansions, forests and castles. Saving precious jewels and scared children from terrible bad guys. I flew jets, rode wild stallions and performed dangerous stunts. I risked my life, ran in front of bullets for others. I was a real hero until I switched off my computer.

Chris Payne (13)

The Car

A man went to a car sales garage, looking for a new car. The attendant showed him around rows of shiny and new cars, like Porsches, Ferraris and Mercedes. Finally the man saw the car he wanted, he wrote out a cheque and was the given the keys to a ... Lada.

Philip Hawkins (14)

Soccer Legend

I've travelled the world. Played in six World Cups. Played against the greatest players of all time. Scored over a hundred goals, played on all the famous turfs, I've been hurt and hurt others but who hasn't?

But now I'm an old, peeling fool. Though I am an old football!

Aden Philpott (14)

Heading For The Line

With speed and pace he tears through the field. Passing one then another. He's passed them all, only one left to beat. The line is in his sights. His heart is pumping and blood rushing as he makes one last dart for his goal, and Irvin takes the chequered flag.

Luke Avron-Cotton (15)

The Lake

Bobbing up and down on the rippling water, so small it looks in the middle of the blue lake. The journey is all in aid of one thing, and that is to catch fish. But the fish aren't around today, so come fish another day, go little grebe, fly away.

Richard Barling

From Riches To Rags

The palace was quite cool, well, cool for an 87-year-old. No loud noise, just groans from next door. But there were 100 bedrooms, all complete with lovely staff to look after you. However, he didn't like the feeling of a hotel; the nursing home was *his* home, after all.

Darren Armstrong (15)

Champion

Don't hit me, it's not worth it. I can't see what it's going to prove if you knock me out. What do you mean it's not going to prove anything? With one almighty punch Lennox Lewis connected and he was Champion of the world, Evander Holyfield lay on the floor.

Paul Gregory (14)

It's A Knockout

There they stand toe to toe, face to face, Lennox Lewis and Mike Tyson. They exchange blows but surely Tyson's winning on points. The bell sounds for round twelve. They touch gloves and the fight starts. Tyson's down, Lewis is victorious. It's official, I am the king of the PlayStation.

Michael Godden (15)

The Submarine

'We've been hit!' the captain shouted. 'All power to main engineering has been cut off and we've lost propulsion! We're sinking deeper and deeper towards the bed.' The man at the helm yelled 'We're gonna die!'

Just as the submarine was going to blow up, Jack pulled the plug out.

Daniel Howard (14)

The Race

'Come on Johnny! Come on, you can do it. Speed it up, that's it, you are doing well. Come on keep going. That's it, you have got what's needed. You have spent ages preparing for this. You are nearly there.'
Finally Johnny got in the car to go to school.

Jacob Brown (14)

The Gunman

'Come on you scum, shoot me if you have the guts,' the man said at point-blank range. He was not showing that he was so scared, he didn't want to move, or his head might get blown to bits. The gunman tensed his finger . . .
and then the power cut out!

Gary Sandy (14)

Flying Needle

It all happens so fast. I have no time to think. I take my strides, then my crossovers and watch it aiming for a hole in the sky. It looks like a flying needle from way down here. Taking its long journey back to solid ground.

Jane Noble (13)

The Jump

'I'm going to do it, stay away, I'm not joking, don't come near me or I'll jump and you won't like me.' 'Please don't jump, you'll kill yourself and if you do jump you will surely land on your neck.' He jumped over the pole and won the Gold Medal.

Carl O'Neill (14)

The Winner And The Loser

He sped up along the dirt track, it was easy for him, he laughed at his steady opponent. The other racer remained at a constant speed. The leader released a little too much! He had lost, the other was the winner. The tortoise was wise, the hare was a fool.

William Lay (13)

Blade And Blood

Sharp, clean and frightening fatal. The knife shimmered in the
neon light, speeding through the thick air. Slicing through the
bloody corpse, crunching, hitting bone, up again (and this time
with greater force) thrusting with all effort.

Teeth gritting, blood spilling,
One leg of lamb Miss, that'll be £2.20.

Andrew Dickson (15)

Is He The One?

She'd always loved him, always would. His brown hair smooth and shiny, his eyes were a sparkling green. On cold nights she'd talk for hours to him, pour her heart out to him, he was always listening, always caring. But, the only words he ever uttered to her were 'Woof.'

Andrew Dickson (15)

Untitled

Bang! The front door closed. A commotion began downstairs. I crept down the stairs to investigate. Eileen, my eldest sister arrived. She was excited and pointed to her wedding finger to explain to me. I screamed a cry of joy, there on her finger sat a small diamond.

Alison McKibben (13)

The Great Battle

He lay on his bed while it ate at his soul, like a ravenous lion. The doctors and nurses in white scuttled around him. His body tried to win the great battle of life and death. But eventually it retreated and the cancer was victorious.

Karen McKee (13)

Untitled

Icy water trickled through my skin. The sun beating down on the crystal water was warm, but I still felt the chill of excitement. The moment was coming, I knew I was in too deep to go back. Then something went wrong, everything went black as body met land.

Sarah McVeigh (13)

Fire

Fire, lots of burning flames, blinding smoke, flashes of red, yellow and orange. Destruction, crumbling bricks, blazing objects, scalding heat, complete loss of control. Then, hoses, filled with water, shooting the building, taming the flames, regaining control. Now, well, all that's left now is a heap of small smouldering ashes.

Elizabeth Patterson (13)

Short Story

Keith's parents' behaviour had been rather odd. They had become miserable people and Keith couldn't do anything. Tropical mango hi-gloss, thought Keith. He did it, Keith painted the fish and chip shop with orange tropical mango paint. His parents still weren't happy. Their mouths were as droopier as ever.

Gemma Mornin (13)

The Race

The people in front seemed so far away. He was sweating from running so long. He got closer and closer, drawing level. Just one more bend. He kept running and running. So close.

He got there just as the bus drew away.

Anne-Marie Pier (12)

The Test

Everyone scribbled on their papers. Except Laura.

'Problem Laura?' questioned Mrs Pieman. Laura bit her lip and hesitated. 'No' she sighed. Laura selected a sharpened pencil and studied the question. After a minute of writing, she replaced the finished crossword on the surgery table.

Holly Neilson (12)

I Wonder

I sometimes wonder what it's like to win a race. Running so fast I couldn't stop. Leading the others, my legs spiralling like windmills out of control.

Reaching the finish line to an eruption of applause and people chanting my name. I will never know for I have no legs.

Lucy Vanes

No More

'He stood staring, staring around him at the things that he would never again be able to see.' Bartholomew knew that he must be punished for the crime that he had so shamefully committed, which was . . .

'That's the end of the lesson now, so no more book till next week.'

April Rose

Mini-Saga

Chasing her with the gun.
Screaming, running down the street.
Hiding behind cars.
People looked on. No one helped.
She can't get away, her legs are not long enough.
He gets too close.
She stops.
Shuts her eyes.
This is it.
He shoots her with the water pistol.

Emma Boyce

Lost And Found

The boy was born in a jungle and was abandoned by his mother. He rose one morning with a gentle touch on his forehead. 'At last it is Mother.' The sound of children echoed round. He squinted his eyes. An image of his mother appeared but licking him was a wolf.

Joanna Moore

Mini-Saga

One drop
Falling to the earth
Tumbling
Twisting
Turning
From above
Slowly, slowly
Then faster and faster
Plummeting towards the ground
The ground draws near
It's going to be too late.

But the parachute springs up
Just in time.

Hayley Mackin (12)

Love Never Dies

They would be together now. Forever. No parents ripping them apart. He mirrored the smile on her dead face with his own. Tears rolled down his cheeks.

He raised the revolver to his temple. He pulled the trigger. Every light in his world went out, except for his beautiful Kathleen.

Dawn Snelling (17)

One-Eyed Sally

'Help, she's dying!' she screamed.
            Down
              The
               Stairs
With   her   beating .... than   electric
             heart   faster   an   pump

'Need to go to the nurse now!' she murmured quickly.

She scrambled towards the nurse.

'Sally's eye has exploded out of her head!'

'Don't worry darling, Mummy will sew it back on tomorrow.'

Laura Brown (11)

Mini-Saga

Quietly walking through the wide corridor
Clanking coming from either side.
Faces pale, depressed.
The warden comes down the corridor
People draw silent
As the wide doors open and school begins.

Elisa Battista (12)

The Storm

Newspapers are flying from every corner, people's hair blows,
trees are swaying and I can feel myself choking.
Am I drowning?
The sun is blocked by a black blanket of clouds.

My eyes fill with tears as the sandstorm rages.

Gemma White

The Race

He ran and ran. He tore around the corner, he gasped.
They overtook him! He ran harder
They were going uphill. He slowed down.
They stopped.
The exchanges took place. He was almost there.
They turned around and went on!
He missed the bus.

Jesse Ryan

The Ghost Story With Another Sense Of Syringe Feeling

Anita was sitting beside the hot blazing fire. Her mother was getting bored, so Anita's mum went into the old broken-down kitchen in the small old building to get a drink.

Anita told her mother a story she heard in school. Her mother was horrified so Anita's mother told her a ghost story.

Anita was getting scared of the thought of the ghost moving around the house unknown and unseen. Anita went to bed very scared but that is another story.

Stephanie Calvely (9)

The Lonely Boy

It was a dark night, a boy was alone in his house and there was a storm. Suddenly everything went off and there were creaks coming from upstairs. The boy went upstairs as quiet as he could. He heard the creaking again. There was nobody in the house at all.

Rachel McKnight (9)

The Boy Who Fell From The Sky And Landed In A Farmer's Cabbage Patch Field

Once there was a boy called Luke who lived with his parents on a hill and Luke's hobby was sky diving. Luke was sky diving and got into difficulty, he fell from the sky and into a cabbage patch.

Luke was lost, he rubbed a cabbage and found himself home again for dinner.

Clare Forehead (9)

Living In America

We were going to live in America. It was a stormy night as we boarded the ship.

Hours later the ship began to sink, the captain told us to get in a lifeboat.

When we were a safe distance the ship went down. Later we were rescued by a ship.

Paul Gault (9)

My Tenth Birthday

My tenth birthday was a birthday to remember, I asked for a bubble couch but couldn't see one in the house until I went upstairs into the bathroom and there it was in the bath. I had a great party. Then watched a video in the evening with my family.

Nicola Gibb (10)

Keeping My Cool

I went to the beach one day, my friends dug a hole in the sand. I climbed in it. They filled it in with my head sticking out to take a photo. A big wave was coming. They were digging and digging, I was panicking, they got me out in time.

Jessica Campbell (10)

The Stealing Orphan

An orphan had to steal food to live. When he tried to steal bread, he was caught and warned not to steal. If he didn't steal, he would die. He got a job as a shoe-shine boy. He didn't steal again and earned money to survive.

Manbir Singh (10)

101 Dalmatians

It all started when Roger married Anita and Pongo married Perdi. Perdi had fifteen pups.

Cruella tried to buy the pups, but couldn't, so she kidnapped them and eighty-three more from pet shops.

They got all the pups back after a few days. They were all adopted by Roger and Anita.

Louise Edwards (10)

Tornado

It came from nowhere, sucking in anything in its path, never to be seen again. It spiralled like a spinning top out of control, it was at least an F5. Somebody had caught it on film. Tommy was the closest. It then stopped when all of the water was gone.

David Breakell (14)

We Can Live Twenty-One Days Without Food, But Only Seven Days Without Water

Tommy's dad is a miner
takes down the pit, one thick sandwich
one bottle cold sweet tea

Tommy helps his dad
makes three sandwiches, two bottles sweetened tea

A roof fall traps Dad below
rescued twelve days later

Kept alive by extra food and tea
by Tommy, his little son.

Glen Thomas

Hostage

A cold sweat is building up. I'm in a near pitch-black room. I'm a hostage. I wish I could get out of here, I'm terrified. I think I could open that window if I tried. But there were footsteps, short, sharp, echoed footsteps. The dentist is ready for me.

Tom Ralph (14)

SUBMISSIONS INVITED

MINI-SAGA INFORMATION

We hope you have enjoyed reading this book and that you will continue to enjoy it in the coming years.

If you would like more details on *Mini-Saga* publications or on how to send in entries then drop us a line or give us a call and we'll be happy to send you a free information pack.

Mark your envelope
Mini-Saga Information
Anchor Books
Forward Press Ltd
Remus House
Peterborough
PE2 9JX

Tel: 01733 898102
Fax: 01733 313524

An Anchor Books Anthology